# 1885-1914
# A NEW INDUSTRY

To commemorate the new 12 mph speed limit the first Emancipation Run to Brighton was held in 1896 and the resort is the once-a-year destination for hundreds of veteran cars such as this 1897 Daimler, built by the first British car manufacturer to sell to the public.

Well, they seem to change their minds pretty frequently, but then if I had a mind like theirs I would change it as soon as I could!'

These words were used about some business associates of his by Dr Frederick William Lanchester, who built the first British four-wheeled petrol-driven car in 1895, when he was twenty-seven. Lanchester has been described as a colossus, a man of imposing stature, and of great intellectual capacity, who was already knowledgeable on aerodynamics and the science of flight before turning to the automobile. The

quotation shows that he was not lacking in wit, either.

Ten years before Lanchester designed and built his first car, with the assistance of his brother George, the German Carl Benz of Mannheim had put a slow-running engine into the rear of a three-wheel chassis, and by 1890 was selling production models to the public. From 1891 he was selling four-wheel versions, and simply because he was the first man to sell cars to the general public, Carl Benz has been credited with 'inventing' the petrol car.

Although Lanchester built the first British petrol-

*Opposite:* The original Wolseley horizontal twin-cylinder three-wheeler of 1896 designed by Herbert Austin.

*Below:* Frederick Lanchester built the first British car in 1895 and his 1896 model had many new engineering features, including a pre-selector gearbox, worm gear drive and forced lubrication, but his ideas were not followed.

driven car, he was not the first British car manufacturer selling production models to the public. The credit for this goes to the Daimler Motor Syndicate of Coventry, founded in 1896 by Harry J. Lawson. Lawson was not an engineer but an entrepreneur. His intention was to control the whole motor industry in England, just as a counterpart in the USA, George B. Selden, tried to control the American motor industry at a later date by cornering all the patents. Neither Lawson nor Selden succeeded in their ambitions, no doubt to the lasting relief of the British and American motor industries.

The Daimler Motor Syndicate derived its name from that of a German called Gottlieb Daimler, of Bad Canstatt, near Stuttgart. Daimler's prominence in the birth of the motor car is due to the fact that he was an engine expert who had patented a 'high-speed' engine in 1885, which was the direct ancestor of the car engines of today, and he had built the first practical four-wheeled petrol-driven car, though it was actually a converted horse-drawn carriage, in 1886. In addition, Daimler's colleague, Wilhelm Maybach, in conjunction with Daimler's son Paul, designed the first Mercedes car just after the turn of the century; it revolutionised car design.

Before that happened, however, the patents for the Daimler engine in France had passed into the hands of Emile Levassor of the firm of Panhard and Levassor. The first 4-cylinder motor-car engines were developed jointly by Daimler and Levassor and were being sold to the public by 1898. Levassor's big contribution to motoring history, however, was his introduction of what was known as the *'systeme Panhard'*. Early in 1891,

# A MOTORING HERITAGE

Maudslay were early innovators, with forced-feed lubrication and overhead valves long before they were common. This 20 hp car had a body to convert from closed landau to open waggonette.

British Leyland has brought together its superb heritage of historic vehicles and put them on permanent display in special halls at Tom Wheatcroft's Donington Collection at Donington Park near Derby.

Initially up to sixty vehicles are to be on display. Many more are available and will be added as and when they are restored.

The collection will consist of motor vehicles, steam rollers, farm machinery, even bicycles, from the past and present companies that today form British Leyland Limited—including Austin, Morris, Wolseley, Riley, Trojan, MG, Triumph. Jaguar, Daimler, Swallow, Lanchester, and the Leyland organisation. This book highlights the fascinating story of the growth of a great industrial power and of the machines that helped build that organisation, from the first steam lawnmower to the latest sports car.

Commercial vehicles   Nick Baldwin
Cars to 1930          Peter Hull
Cars from 1930        John McLellan

Editor: John McLellan

Many ex-First World War 40 hp
Maudslays worked through the 'twenties
on their solid tyres.

# A MOTORING HERITAGE

John Bartholomew & Son Limited · Edinburgh and London
*in association with*
Leyland Historic Vehicles Limited

# CONTENTS

*First published in Great Britain* 1976 *by*
**John Bartholomew & Son Limited**
12 Duncan Street, Edinburgh EH9 1TA
And at 216 High Street, Bromley BR1 1PW

*in association with*
**Leyland Historic Vehicles Limited**
174 Marylebone Road, London
© John Bartholomew & Son Limited and Leyland Historic Vehicles Limited, 1976

ISBN 0 7028 1065 7

Designed by Melvyn Gill Design Associates Limited
Printed in Great Britain by Hazell Watson & Viney, Aylesbury, Buckinghamshire

being impressed with Daimler's engines, but not his cars, which were like horse-drawn carriages with central pivot front axles fitted with engines at the rear, Levassor, after early experiments with rear engines, designed cars having a V twin-cylinder Daimler engine at the front of a wooden chassis, with the crankshaft in the longitudinal axis, driving through a foot-controlled friction clutch to a sliding pinion gearbox, and thence to the rear wheels via a countershaft and final chain drive. This was the forerunner of the cars of the future and Levassor proved its effectiveness in early motor races.

The British Daimlers produced in a huge disused cotton mill in Coventry, known as the 'Motor Mills' were, in fact, copies of Panhard-Levassors, although being rather well made they were heavier than their French counterparts, and had less performance. Gottlieb Daimler was a director of the firm, but had no hand in the products. Also made under the same roof were cars called MMCs (Motor Manufacturing Co.), which were almost indistinguishable from Daimlers.

By now the leaders in automobile design were the French and not the Germans. In England the motor car was not encouraged. Until an Act was passed in 1896 the speed limit was 4 mph and a man was supposed to walk in front of every motor car, although his obligation to wave a red flag at the same time had been rescinded in 1878. Yet by now full-scale motor races had been held in France and Emile Levassor in 1895 had won the 732-mile Paris—Bordeaux—Paris race on a 2-cylinder Panhard at an average speed of 15 mph, driving single-handed for 48 hours 48 minutes.

An Act of 1896 put the speed limit up to 12 mph, and on Saturday, 14 November of that year some 20 to 30 cars took part in an 'Emancipation Run' from London to

Shown in Hon. John Scott Montagu's Daimler four-cylinder, Edward VII was a keen motoring supporter.

Typical veteran-car detail on Wolseley; note chain drive to rear axle, sprag in case brakes do not hold car if it stalls on hill, and wooden-spoked wheels with solid tyres. Herbert Austin developed his original horizontal-engined designs and they put up the best performances by British cars in the 1904-05 Gordon Bennett races. But design was heading in the direction pointed by Continental cars such as the Mercedes and horizontal engines lost favour. Austin went on to build cars under his own name.

Brighton, led by H.J.Lawson, founder of the Motor Car Club. Panhard was the predominant make in the Run, and Lawson and his wife were driven in the Panhard that had won the Paris—Bordeaux—Paris race.

In view of the technical lead held by the French, it is hardly surprising that when the British started making cars themselves, they either copied the French cars, or else imported them from the Continent and sold them under an English name.

One of the most important of these early firms was Wolseley, and their designer bore one of the most famous names in British motoring history—Austin. Herbert Austin, born in 1866 and educated in Rotherham, Yorkshire, was apprenticed to the Great Northern Railway Company. As a young man he went out to Australia and took a job with the Wolseley Sheep-Shearing Co Ltd. In 1889 an English factory was established in Birmingham, and in 1893 Austin returned to England to work there as production manager, where bicycles and textile machinery were made as well as the sheep-shearing machines.

He became interested in the possibility of manufacturing motor cars and went to Paris to investigate progress in design. He decided to build a car on the lines of the Leon Bollee tricar, but instead of the Bollee's horizontal single-cylinder engine, with his own air-cooled flat twin-cylinder engine, which he completed in 1895. This engine, carried longitudinally on the nearside of the frame was most remarkable for its valve gear, which was overhead, and operated by an overhead camshaft driven by a vertical shaft and skew gearing. At this time most cars had automatic inlet valves, opened by the suction of the descending piston and kept on their seat by a light spring.

As his first car infringed some Bollee patents, Austin built a second three-wheeler, which did not have two wheels at the front and a single one at the back like the Bollee and his first tricar. Instead, he put the two wheels at the back. The engine was now a horizontal single cylinder with a conventional, for the time,

*Right:* R.W.Maudslay started the Standard company to build cars with fully interchangeable (standardised) parts. Their first 1903 car was designed by Alex Craig, responsible for Maudslay design, and had an under-floor single-cylinder engine.

*Left:* By 1907 Standard had become more conventional, but were early in offering six-cylinder engines. This 30 hp tourer is typical of their quite inexpensive range.

*Right:* Rovers made an early name for themselves with the robust and well-made single-cylinder models of 6 and 8 hp. This is a very typical example with its roomy two-seater body and low bonnet.

*Below:* The London Motor Show was the sales battleground and manufacturers such as Wolseley showed superbly-crafted cars each year at Olympia.

*Above:* Rover also succeeded in the increasingly important medium-price and medium-size market with the 20 hp four, which won the Isle of Man TT race in 1907 driven by Courtis. The shield design was to be a Rover feature for decades.

automatic-inlet valve, and was air-cooled. This model went into limited production and was one of the very first cars of 100 per cent British design and manufacture to be offered to the public. Rather amazingly, both of these original Wolseleys are still preserved in the Leyland Historic Vehicle collection.

In 1899 there followed the first Wolseley four-wheeled car, still designed by Austin, known as the Wolseley Voiturette. This had a front-mounted single-cylinder horizontal water-cooled engine rated at 3 hp, tiller steering, and drive by belt to a 3-speed gearbox, with final drive by side chains.

This car, which is also miraculously preserved today, and has done several long trips in recent years, put up a remarkably good performance when driven by its designer in the British 1,000 Miles Trial of April—May 1900, although some weaknesses in the belt drive were shown up, and in production models Austin replaced the belt with a friction clutch and internally-toothed chain-drive from engine to gearbox.

*Above:* In the late-Edwardian era coachbuilders achieved a level of craftsmanship and sumptuousness hardly to be exceeded and this Wolseley limousine is a good example. Tyres were of larger section to improve the ride for this high-powered luxury car.

*Left:* This Wolseley of barely a decade before underlines what great strides were being made. In this rear-entrance tonneau body all the occupants were exposed to the weather and with a full load performance was substantially reduced.

From 1900 the Lanchester brothers began to manufacture their cars in Birmingham, where they had established the Lanchester Engine Co. in 1895. The design of the Lanchester car owed practically nothing to any other make, as Frederick Lanchester designed it entirely from first principles, having decided that the general trend of motor car engineering practice was thoroughly unscientific. Lanchester was one of the first people to pay attention to the chassis of the motor car as regards ride comfort and handling, and to get away from the 'horseless carriage' aspect of putting an engine into any old carriage that happened to be handy. He was also fussy about engine balance and smoothness. The first production Lanchester had full cantilever springs, a fully-balanced horizontally-opposed engine set amidships with forced-draught cooling, epicyclic gearbox, and worm drive to the live back axle. Lanchester was happy to incorporate tiller steering, which on other cars was going out in favour of the steering wheel, and he used splined instead of

squared shafts, a considerable refinement.

If Lanchester never copied anybody else, nobody copied him, so his ideas were not generally adopted. He was far ahead of his time, but he had other interests and did not devote himself entirely to perfecting his own motor cars, this task falling more to his brother George. He was also content that his early cars should not travel very much faster than horse-drawn traffic, so that by the time of the 1900 1,000 Miles Trial the Lanchesters were rather lacking in performance in comparison with their rivals, and as an instance, the 8 hp Lanchester was outpaced by Austin's 3 hp Wolseley Voiturette. This was corrected on later Lanchester models.

Two other firms becoming active at this time were Star and Riley, and both were in the cycle industry.

Stars were made in Wolverhampton by the Lisle family, owners of the Star Cycle Co., and they produced their first car in 1898 and offered it for sale the following year. It copied the Benz. Later French De Dion engines were used, and larger models were based first on Panhard, then Mercedes design.

Riley of Coventry was another family business,

which had started by manufacturing weaving equipment, and then transferred to bicycles. In 1899, at the National Cycle Show at the Crystal Palace, they had shown their Royal Riley quadricycle, with a 2½ hp De Dion engine. This had four wheels, but was built on bicycle lines, with a saddle, handlebars, a forecar-type passenger's seat out at the front, and pedalling gear.

One of the senior members of the family, William Riley, had four talented sons, Victor, Stanley, Allen and Percy: Percy proved to be the engineering genius and not long after leaving school built himself a car over a period of two years, completing it in 1898. It had a front-mounted vertical single-cylinder engine and belt drive, and was notable for incorporating a mechanically-operated inlet valve. This prototype never went into production, but was used in and around Coventry for several years. It was not until 1905 that Rileys produced another four-wheeled car, and until 1907 produced successful tricars, later examples of which had proper bodywork, with a seat replacing the driver's saddle, and a steering wheel replacing the handlebars.

In 1903 R.W.Maudslay founded the Standard Motor Co. in Coventry. Presumably he was a civil engineer

*Above:* Rover kept their motor-cycle interests going after returning to the market with the excellent 1911 3½ hp machine. Here a road-equipped example poses in the Brooklands paddock, its acetylene headlamp a feature.

having been engaged in the construction of Barry Dock, near Cardiff, and certainly he appointed a mechanical engineer called Alex Craig to design the first Standard car. This had an 'over-square' single cylinder engine, located under the floor. The name Standard was chosen because the intention was to build a limited number of inexpensive cars with as many standardised and interchangeable parts as possible.

Crossley Brothers Ltd, of Gorton, Manchester, were one of the oldest makers of internal combustion engines in the country, having built four-stroke engines under licence from the pioneers Otto and Langen of Deutz. Gottlieb Daimler had himself worked for Crossley when he spent a short period in England in 1862; and later on, when they started making Daimler engines, he acted as consultant to them. Towards the end of 1903 Crossley brought out their first car. Designed by J.S.Critchley, formerly of Daimler in Coventry, it was a 22 hp chain-driven four-cylinder. The design was of Mercedes inspiration and, apart from the engine, the car was largely made up of imported parts. This was followed by a similar 28 hp model, but by 1906 a 40 hp car of completely British construction was produced, although the design was inspired by the Italian FIAT, which itself owed much to Mercedes.

J.K.Starley had been building penny-farthing bicycles in Coventry as early as 1877, and in 1884 was one of the pioneers of the 'safety bicycle', which has changed so little right up to the present day. He produced these Rover bicycles in large quantities. In 1889 Starley built an experimental motorised tricycle, but it was not until 1903 that his company marketed a few 2¼ hp motor cycles.

The first Rover car appeared in 1904, an 8 hp single-cylinder with the water-cooled engine at the front and an interesting tubular backbone frame of advanced design making much use of aluminium. Initially the 8 hp Rover had an unsprung back axle, which was definitely not advanced, but before long a more conventional ash frame with reinforced flitch plates (known as an 'armoured chassis') replaced the backbone construction, and a sprung back axle was fitted. The original wire-and-bobbin steering was replaced by rack and pinion, the latter having been an 'optional extra' on the early cars. There was a '3-speed and reverse' gearbox with a steering-column gear-change, and the 'Rover patent automatic' carburettor, under the floor a long way from the engine, meant that there was a new feature—an accelerator pedal.

All petrol engines up to 1900 had been single speed, the revs only being slightly varied by use of air and ignition controls, thus gear changing had to be used not only when getting away from rest or when climbing hills as it is today, but also to vary speed on the level or in traffic.

The 8 hp Rover gave some 40 mpg and maximum speeds in the three gears were 8, 16 and 24 mph. For those who found these speeds too hectic, the makers produced a 6 hp version as they feared the 8 hp might be 'too powerful' for the less steely nerved. An interesting feature was a 'camshaft brake', whereby movement of the footbrake moved the camshaft and altered the valve timing so that the engine could be used as a brake. This arrangement also appeared on the 16/20 hp 4-cylinder Rovers of 1906. The 6 and 8 hp cars were designed by E.W.Lewis who, like J.S.Critchley, the Crossley designer, also came from Daimler.

Edwardian cars owed a great deal to the design of the first Mercedes of 1901 with its low-slung chassis, honeycomb radiator, gate change, magneto ignition, mechanical inlet valves and efficient carburettor—the first 'modern' car and a credit to its German designers, Wilhelm Maybach and Paul Daimler.

Herbert Austin was a keen supporter of motor racing and horizontal engines, and himself drove racing Wolseleys (which unfortunately retired) in the 1902 Paris—Vienna and 1903 Paris—Madrid races. His most successful racing cars, which put up the best British performance in the 1904/5 Gordon Bennett races, were the Wolseley 'Beetles', so called because of their beetle-like bonnets, which had 12-litre engines carried transversely across the chassis, with their four horizontal cylinders ahead of the crankshaft. Austin had a row with the Wolseley management over his stubborn insistence on the fitting of horizontal engines, and after resigning from Wolseleys in the autumn of 1905, began manufacturing Austin cars in an old printing works in Birmingham in 1906. To these cars he promptly fitted vertical engines. Austin had links with the French Clement firm, and his side-valve production cars, as well as his 9½-litre 1908 Grand Prix cars, followed Clement design. In the 1908 French Grand Prix at Dieppe, J.T.C.Moore-Brabazon, later Lord Brabazon, and Dario Resta finished eighteenth and nineteenth respectively at just over 54 mph after over 8½-hours racing in these Austins, one of which still survives, with its 4-cylinder 127 × 127 mm T-head side-valve engine.

William R. Morris, one time Oxford bicycle repairer and racer, was eleven years younger than Herbert Austin, and had produced motor cycles before launching his first car, the Morris Oxford, in 1913. This was a thoroughly good car, made up in a former military academy in Cowley, Oxford, from proprietary parts, of which the main component was a T-head 1-litre four-cylinder White and Poppe engine. The 1½-litre Morris Cowley of 1915 was inspired by a visit by Morris to Detroit and was mostly American, having a side-valve Continental engine, a 3-speed gearbox made by Detroit Gear, and axles and steering of imported U.S. components. A thousand Morris Oxfords were sold by 1914, but Morris's story really belongs to the postwar period.

Daimler sales declined in 1900—02 as the cars lacked performance in comparison with their rivals. Thenceforth the firm built increasingly powerful cars, driven by noisy side chains, until Frederick Lanchester was called in as Consulting Engineer to cure crankshaft failures on six-cylinder models, which he did by inventing the Lanchester vibration-damper, afterwards much used by other makes. He also persuaded the firm to unshackle their chains and fit live-axle transmission incorporating the Lanchester 'hour glass' worm gear. The chain-drive cars did well in hill climbs and sprints, but after 1909 all Daimlers were fitted with Knight double-sleeve-valve engines. In 1910 Daimler was taken over by the BSA (Birmingham Small Arms) armaments group. The first Royal order for a Daimler had been received in 1898 when Edward VII was still Prince of Wales, and latterly the name became synonymous with vast limousines, for long used by royalty.

During Herbert Austin's time, Wolseley had become a subsidiary of Vickers, another armaments firm, and after Austin left, J.D.Siddeley designed vertical-engined cars that were called Wolseley-Siddeleys. At first these had inlet-over-exhaust valve engines, but by 1908 L-head side-valve engines were standard, and no more chain-drive cars were made. Siddeley went to the Deasy firm in 1909, where E.W.Lewis was designing Rover-like cars, and his name was not linked with Wolseley from 1911. By 1914 Wolseley were offering four- and six-cylinder cars, and an excellent light car called the Stellite, which was actually made to

*Above:* Percy Lambert's Brooklands racing 20 hp Austin Pearley III, which had many successes.

*Below:* Morris Oxfords lined up in 1913 outside the Cowley factory.

Wolseley designs by another Vickers subsidiary as there was not the room in the Wolseley works to produce it.

Within the Lanchester fold, the first vertical four-cylinder engine was introduced in 1904, and it was moved forward between the dashboard and the front seat between the driver and passenger, as on a forward drive truck. The twin-cylinder cars faded out, a 28 hp six-cylinder came out in 1906, to be replaced by a 38 hp in 1911, and a 25 hp four-cylinder replaced the 20 hp in 1912.

The last pre-war Lanchester, the Sporting 40 of 1914, was the work of George Lanchester, and was a fair bid to rival the Rolls-Royce. It was the first Lanchester to have the engine in a conventional position covered by a normal bonnet, and its 5.6-litre six-cylinder engine with side-valves was in unit with a three-speed epicyclic gearbox. The springs were underslung, and naturally it kept the traditional silent worm drive, but few examples were made.

Rileys at Coventry brought out their first production four-wheeled car in 1905, the 9 hp V-twin with its amidships engine taken from the tricar, and they were successful in hill climbs and sprints in 1906 and 1907. A bigger 12—18 hp twin followed with a round radiator and conventionally-sited engine. Riley were doing very well making their patent detachable wheels, which were naturally fitted to their own cars, as well as to Mercedes, Rolls-Royce, Hispano-Suiza, Napier, Panhard, Renault, and the record-breaking Blitzen Benz. Just before the war the 17-30 Riley appeared, with a four-cylinder-in-line side-valve 3-litre engine, with the now familiar round radiator, but Riley's great days were ahead.

The Star Company in Wolverhampton, meanwhile, went from strength to strength with well-made, rather expensive, but conventional cars. Star could not make up their minds what to call their cheaper line of small cars. At first they called them Starlings, then Stuarts, and finally a separate company was formed to manufacture them under the name of Briton. Star became one of the six largest car manufacturers in Britain before the Great War.

Crossley stuck to four-cylinder models until the 'twenties, and had most success after the car division was separated from the engine company in 1910 and William Letts was appointed managing director. With his partner Charles Jarrott he had long marketed Crossleys. Designed by A.W.Reeves the 4-litre 20 hp Crossley was a very popular car, and, as the 20/25 hp, became famous as a staff car and tender to the Royal Flying Corps during the Great War. A side-valve 15 hp model distinguished itself at Shelsley Walsh Hill Climb, and heralded the production of the 15 hp Shelsley Crossley just before the war, an example of which ran in the 1914 TT.

R.W.Maudslay himself drove a 16 hp four-cylinder Standard non-stop to eleventh place in the 1905 Tourist Trophy race in the Isle of Man, and Edwardian Standards did well in trials and hill climbs. Both 24/30 hp and 15 hp side-valve six-cylinder models were successful up to 1914, and there was a 50 hp luxury model as well as a 9,5 hp light car introduced in 1913.

A Rover won the Isle of Man 241-mile Tourist Trophy race in 1907 in continuous rain at 28.8 mph, driven by Ernest Courtis. This was the 4-cylinder 16/20 hp. The 6 and 8 hp single-cylinder Rovers were made until 1912, when Owen Clegg from Wolseleys designed an excellent 12 hp four-cylinder 2.2-litre side-valve model with a carburettor made under licence from SU, and worm final drive. Some of the features from this model were put into cars Clegg designed for Darracq, his next port of call. For 1911 Rovers made some sleeve-valve single- and twin-cylinder cars, but few were sold. During the war Rover built 12/16 hp Sunbeam cars under licence, to which they fitted taller, narrower radiators, for War Office use in France.

# COMMERCIAL VEHICLES

Leyland had the distinction of being one of the oldest commercial vehicle makers in the world. An eighty-year process of takeover and amalgamation has made it by far the largest British-owned truck and bus producer.

Most of the takeovers and mergers of the 'fifties and 'sixties involved many other companies with fascinating backgrounds. In this brief look at their highspots and histories it should be remembered that many of the events described took place when the various firms that are now the British Leyland Truck and Bus and Special Products Groups were in fact competitors. AEC, Maudslay, and Crossley formally joined forces in

1948 and took over Thornycroft in 1961; Leyland acquired Albion in 1951 and Scammell in 1955 and then took over AEC in 1962. This greatly enlarged Leyland group then joined forces with British Motor Holdings in 1968 and thus acquired several former heavy-vehicle makers like Austin, Wolseley, Morris, Guy, and Alvis.

In covering British Leyland's commercial-vehicle interests it is impossible to mention all the light vans and trucks based on their car chassis; just about every company now involved in the Leyland group has made commercial vehicles in one form or another in the past.

Chain-drive and oil lamps for this Albion tanker.

*Right:* Built in 1902, an early Albion commercial vehicle was the A2. It had an 8 hp petrol engine and a 10 cwt capacity. Wheels were wooden spoked and solid tyred.

*Below:* The Pig was the nickname for Leyland's first petrol-engined lorry of 1904. With 30 cwt capacity it had a live rear axle and led to the successful 24 hp Y-series 3 ton model of 1905.

The honour of producing the first practical goods' vehicle in Britain is almost equally divided between Leyland and Thornycroft. Both models were powered by steam and appeared in 1896. Strangely enough, though the Lancashire Steam Motor Company (Leyland's forerunners) continued to produce steam vehicles for many years and took over Coulthards, another local manufacturer, both they and Thornycroft devoted most of their energies after the first few years to petrol-driven vehicles. Luckily a handful of very early Thornycroft steamers have survived and an example can be seen at Donington as well as a 1919 Leyland that spent its working life in Australia.

Not surprisingly Daimler of Coventry, holders of important German petrol-engine patents in this country, were staunch advocates of internal combustion and their first petrol-driven commercial vehicles were introduced in 1896—7, though a few were imported before that date from Germany and France.

Wolseley dates from the Victorian era. Their forward-control goods and passenger vehicles were popular in Edwardian times, though these were gradually discontinued in favour of cars, with a brief resurgence of interest in heavy vehicles during the First World War.

Albion, Crossley, Maudslay, Star, Standard, Austin, and Rover all came into being in the first few years of the century and all were primarily car makers, although commercial vehicles at Albion and Maudslay gradually replaced car production by the time of the Great War. Except for essential purposes, few cars were produced in Britain between 1914 and 1918 and most manufacturers switched to armaments or else concentrated on military vehicles. Thus Austin with their unusual 2-ton chassis, in which drive was taken to each rear wheel hub by a separate propeller shaft, Crossley, Wolseley, Daimler, Lanchester, and Star all made lorries or tenders. Rover helped to manufacture Maudslay's unusual three-tonners, which featured the Maudslay speciality of overhead-camshaft engines, which they had pioneered in 1902 and which, updated,

*Below:* As early as 1898 Thornycroft designed an articulated steam wagon outfit that was awarded War Office approval when it was demonstrated at the Liverpool trials. It was driven by chain.

were still available in 1949. Albion, Leyland, and Thornycroft were all major heavy-vehicle makers in the years before the Great War, with thriving exports and a growing home market as the benefits of motor — as opposed to horse haulage — became apparent. Fortunately a fine example of a heavy vehicle of this time has survived in the form of a Leyland X-type.

AEC was solely a bus maker until 1915 and up until 1912 had been the manufacturing plant for an important group of London bus operators. They had decided that they could produce the ideal vehicle for their particular requirements and from various earlier experimental and production buses the immortal B-type was born in 1910. This was a remarkably lightweight 34-seat double-decker that dispensed with the almost universal chain drive of the time, but had the archaic, yet effective, wood and steel sandwich chassis.

In 1912 the Associated Equipment Company (AEC) was formed as an independent subsidiary of the London General Omnibus Company. Although it was primarily involved with producing vehicles for the London General Omnibus Company, AEC began to look further afield and appointed Daimler as its provincial sales outlet. Only a small number of AECs had been handled by Daimler when war was declared and soon the whole of AEC's output was geared to the war effort. They evolved the steel-chassis Y-type three-tonner for the War Department, and with the help of the first moving-track assembly line for heavy vehicles in Europe, possibly the world, produced a staggering total of 10,000 lorries in the five years of war. Many Y-chassis went to Daimler of Coventry to be fitted with Daimler's Knight-sleeve valve engine.

Thus AEC were the largest British suppliers of commercial vehicles to the war effort, though Leyland, with their RAF-type (supplied mainly to the RFC/RAF), Thornycroft with their J, and Albion with their chain drive A and B models were not far behind, with approximately 5,000—6,000 vehicles each. Lanchester supplied armoured cars.

# 1919-1929 THE YEARS OF GROWTH

Possibly the most significant of all British cars of this period, the Austin Seven of 1922 opened a new era in motoring for owners who previously would have been exposed to the elements on motor cycles or suffered the crudities of cyclecars.

The Great War was followed by a boom, during which almost any car could be sold, particularly if it was cheap, but the boom was inevitably followed by a slump. Rovers got in on the cheap-car market with the introduction of the Rover Eight, for which the slogan ran 'You cannot over rate the Rover Eight!' This rather crude but quite effective little car had an 8 hp flat twin aircooled engine, of which it is said the cylinder heads glowed cherry red at night. Two-seater bodywork was standard, springing was quarter elliptic and steering rack and pinion, and the fact that it had the customary Rover worm final drive to its 3-speed transmission instead of chain just prevented it being classed as a cyclecar. It continued until 1925, when the four-cylinder o.h.v. water-cooled 9/20 took over, followed by the 1.2 litre 10/25 hp. More interesting were the four-cylinder overhead camshaft 14/45 and 16/50 cars of 1925 and 1926 respectively, with engines designed by P.A.Poppe of White and Poppe, the 14/45 winning the RAC's Dewar Trophy for 50 consecutive ascents of Bwlch-y-Gross. Less expensive to make was the 2-litre push-rod ohv six-cylinder, with spiral bevel final drive, an example of which beat the Blue Train from St Raphael to Calais in 1930.

Herbert Austin's way of meeting the depression was to produce the immortal Austin Seven, or Baby Austin, which effectively put all the cyclecar firms out of business. It was successful simply because it was so good. It pulled the Austin Company out of financial doldrums, although the contemporary 20 hp and the Twelve-four were also good cars, particularly the latter, better than the six-cylinder 'Twenty' and 'Sixteen' produced towards the end of the vintage period. Not

Many coachbuilders built bodies for the Austin Seven. This is a Swallow version of 1930—31, designed by William Lyons.

*Right:* For all its merits, the Bean car could not withstand Morris's determined price-cutting. One of their last products was the 18/50 Six of 1928 with its Meadows engine.

*Left:* Just after the First World War many luxury cars appeared on the market using technology obtained during the conflict. Parry Thomas's Leyland Eight was one of the greatest. A change of policy by Leyland management ensured few were built but features of the design lived on in Leyland's commercial vehicles.

*Right:* The Austin Twelve was a long-lived and profitable car. Its side-valve engine and basic chassis design was used for London taxis for generations. The company was influenced by American ideas when the car was introduced. This is a 1922 tourer.

only did developments of the little side-valve Austin Seven achieve many racing successes, but the cars were made under licence all over the world, where they sold under different names—Rosengart in France, Dixi in Germany, Bantam in the USA, and Datsun in Japan, for example.

William Morris prospered by actually reducing his prices in 1921 to surmount the slump through in-creased sales, though his profit came down to £15 per car. As the Continental engines were no longer avail-able from the USA, Morris had copies of them made for him by the Hotchkiss Factory in Coventry. By the end of 1922 he had absorbed his radiator suppliers, Osberton Radiators, and Hollick and Pratt of Coventry, who made his bodies. In 1923 the Hotchkiss factory became his, as well as Wrigley, who made his gear-

*Above:* Enthusiasts have always tuned popular family cars. The Bullnose Morris-based special was built by H.R.Wellsteed and raced at Brooklands in 1926—28, putting in a standing lap at 78 mph driven by C.Paul.

*Right:* Continental coachwork tastes can be seen in this Wolseley of the 'twenties, with its fabric-covered body and small boot. The Riley Nine Monaco of 1926 was in a similar touring-saloon style.

*Below:* Vanden Plas built the Brougham coachwork on this 1923—24 21 hp Lanchester. Presence of a windscreen wiper is notable.

boxes and back axles, whilst in 1927 he took over the SU carburettor firm.

At first the bullnose Morris Cowley was merely a cheap edition of the Oxford, but in 1925 the latter was given a larger-bore engine.

The Wolseley Company had made overhead camshaft Hispano-Suiza aero engines during the war, and went on to produce cars with single-overhead-camshaft engines as well as with side-valves. In 1927 Wolseley Motors was acquired by Morris, who then began to fit single ohc engines to some of his products,

the 2½-litre Morris Isis Six of 1928 being based on the Wolseley 16/45. The single ohc Morris Minor of 1928 was intended to rival the Austin Seven, but the Seven was too firmly established to be usurped by a car that really had little more to offer. A small six, the Wolseley Hornet of 1930, sold well, and has been described as a Morris Minor with two extra cylinders.

The other spin-off from the Morris, and a much more important one, was the MG. These were sports cars based on Morris designs and produced originally at Morris Garages under Cecil Kimber. Following the

*Below left:* The late-'twenties Crossley six-cylinder possessed excellent brakes and well executed saloon bodywork.

*Above:* The 1927 Daimler stand at Olympia included an example of the sleeve-valve Double-Six V12 model.

*Below right:* Vanden Plas were leaders in the luxury-formal body field and this limousine demonstrates their careful attention to detail.

Morris idiom, there were 'bullnose' and the 'flatnose' 14/40 MGs with side-valve engines and lightened engine internals. There was the very fine ohc 18/80 with a much modified version of the Isis engine, but it was the inexpensive M-type MG Midget, based on the Morris Minor, which became a runaway success, both on road and track, in the early 'thirties.

Another remarkable car of the vintage decade was the Riley Nine. After the war Riley made a few 17—30 hp cars and then a very good four-cylinder side-valve 1½-litre designed by Harry Rush, which became known in sports form as the Redwing. In 1926 Percy Riley's 9 hp was introduced, with the famous Monaco-fabric saloon body. The great feature of its four-cylinder engine was its hemispherical combustion chambers, with the valves operated by two high-set camshafts via very short, and therefore light, pushrods, which combined most of the virtues of a twin overhead-camshaft engine whilst avoiding its snags so far as maintenance was concerned. With the Austin Seven, the Riley Nine was one of the outstanding British designs of its period. In its Brooklands form, as

*Above:* The Swallow coachworks were still turning out sidecars in 1929 at the Foleshill, Coventry factory, while special bodies on a range of Austin, Standard and Fiat chassis were also in hand.

*Right:* Standard's 1926 Charlecote 14 hp tourer is very typical of British practice in the late-'twenties, with its robust four-cylinder engine and practical two-seater drophead bodywork with sliding windows.

developed by Reid Railton and J.G.Parry Thomas, it was the nucleus of many successful sports and racing cars with both four- and six-cylinder engines.

Star went into financial decline during the vintage years, when they built good if rather conservative cars, and latterly probably too many models. In 1928 they were taken over by Guy, the Wolverhampton commercial-vehicle firm, who had themselves made a few luxury V8 and 4-cylinder cars between 1919 and 1925. Star cars did not last long after the end of the Vintage period.

Crossley in Manchester survived the Vintage period when they, too, built some good cars, and in the early years assembled not only American Overlands, but also a few French Bugattis. They went over to building commercial vehicles in the 'thirties, in the early years of

which their 2-litre engine powered the 16/80 Lagonda sports car.

In 1919 Standard built an enlarged version of their 1913 9.5 hp Rhyl model, but the 13.9 hp SLO4 with overhead valves and worm drive was their most successful model by 1925. When finances became difficult, the cheap 4-cylinder side-valve worm-drive Nine with fabric bodywork came out in 1928. Bigger side-valve six-cylinder models followed in 1930, and the appearance of William Lyons's special Swallow bodies fitted to Standard chassis was to have enormous repercussions, not so much on Standards, but on the future of the Swallow Coachbuilding Co. Ltd, which had started by making sidecars in Blackpool in 1921.

Beans engineering shops and foundries at Tipton, Staffs, today produce castings for British Leyland where A. Harper Sons & Bean Ltd were operating a foundry as long ago as 1826. As motor-component makers after the Great War they were members of a consortium that attempted to mass-produce a car called the Bean. They rather overdid the cost cutting, but although one model, the Fourteen, introduced in 1924, was a good design, the sheer ruggedness, which was the main virtue of the lesser models, was not enough, and the last car was produced in 1929. In the thirties Beans Industries at Tipton built George Eyston's land speed record car 'Thunderbolt' as well as the front axles for ERA racing cars, and the Gough-designed engines for chain-driven Frazer Nash sports cars.

One of the great luxury cars of the 'twenties was George Lanchester's Forty, a development of the pre-war Sporting Forty, but now with a single-overhead-camshaft straight-eight engine of 6.2 litres, which gave it a fine performance. In 1923 came a scaled-down version of the Forty, the 21 hp, which, to keep costs down, went against Lanchester tradition by having a conventional gearbox instead of an epicyclic. In 1928 came the last true Lanchester before their merger with Daimler and the BSA group, this being a straight Eight 30, in effect a 21 hp with two extra cylinders. Lanchester was one of several distinguished makers that did not survive the depression of 1929—31.

BSA supplemented motor cycles with a light car soon after the war; it had an air-cooled V-twin engine of 1080 cc made by the Hotchkiss factory at Coventry, but this engine was discontinued when the factory was taken over by Morris, and until it too was abandoned in 1926, the BSA car had a sleeve-valve engine from the smallest Daimler. Daimler themselves, with sleeve-valves and worm-drive rear axles, prospered during the 'twenties with a bewilderingly large number of models from an underpowered 12 hp to an impressive V12 Double Six, but they remained conservative, if not archaic, in their detail fittings and were very much chauffeurs' cars.

The Leyland commercial-vehicle company made a foray into private-car manufacture in the 'twenties with a very expensive car and a very cheap one. The 90 mph luxury car was the Leyland Eight of 1920, with a straight eight 7.2-litre single-overhead-camshaft engine having cantilever springs to close the valves. Only about eighteen of these cars were made, and the designer, J.G. Parry Thomas, developed one example into a single-seater Brooklands racing car with which he took the lap record at 129.36 mph in 1925. Only one Leyland Eight survives, with its anti-roll bars front and rear and quarter elliptic leaf springs at the back mounted on torsion bars inside the frame, and this sporting two-seater was built up from parts in 1929. The cheap car was the remarkable Trojan, with a two-stroke engine under the front seats having two double cylinders each pair coupled by a communal head, a 2-speed epicyclic gearbox, suspension by long cantilever springs, and solid tyres. This unique car was cheaper than the Austin Seven as well as roomier, although it would only do 38 mph. It had every virtue but looks and performance, and was a success. A Trojan once seen was never forgotten.

First Alvis was the side-valve 10/30 of 1920. There were no front-wheel brakes and the beetle-backed body was forerunner of handsome beetle-and duck's-back sports bodies seen on the famous 12/50 model of a few seasons later.

# HISTORIC BIKES

Although motor cycles have long ceased to be an important part of the motor industry in Britain, for many years they provided useful income for their parent companies. Triumph, in particular, with a fine range of machines, helped the car building side of the business through hard times in the late 'twenties and 'thirties before the motor cycle interests were finally sold off.

Racing and competition were always important to the motor cyclist and the fine collection of awards for racing in the TTs and at Brooklands, as well as in reliability trials, testify to the sound design and reliability of makes such as Rover, Triumph and BSA.

**1** The original 3½ hp Rover motor cycle of 1911 was belt driven and had cycle type caliper front brakes.

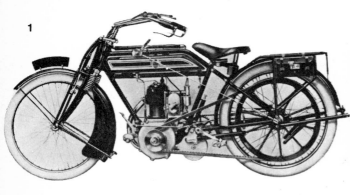

**4**

**5**

RY 6019

**6**

DR 8609

**7**

**8**

FR 3030

**2** Also belt driven, this 3½ hp Triumph was ridden by Jack Marshall to victory in the 1908 Tourist Trophy race in the Isle of Man at 40.4 mph average.

**3** Triumph proved the pace and reliability of their products when I.B.Hart-Davies rode a 1909 model over the 886 miles between Lands End and John O'Groats in 33 hr 22 min.

**4** For those who felt that the upkeep and running costs of a car were too heavy, the sidecar outfit was an alternative. This Triumph Gloria of 1923 has a luxurious coachbuilt touring sidecar.

**5** BSA were one of the great British names, with a range running from touring to sports machines. This 1928 'Sloper' ohv single is a good example of designs that took them healthily into the 'thirties.

**6** Lightweight bikes were always a BSA speciality and this 1925 sv was popular.

**7** High performance was offered by this sv BSA big twin of 1925.

**8** In his earlier years, Sir William Lyons was a keen motor cycle sportsman. Here he is riding a Harley Davidson twin from USA in full racing trim.

*Above:* The side-valve Austin Sevens still dominated 750 cc racing as the 1920s closed. Here the 'Dutch clog' racers get away at the start of the 500 miles race at Brooklands in 1931.

*Below:* The Alvis front-wheel drive cars won their class in the 1928 Le Mans 24 Hour Race. Basically a sound design, the fwd cars were possibly introduced before motoring opinion was ready

One of the great sports cars of the 'twenties was the Alvis, the firm having been founded in Coventry in 1919 by T.G.John, and few firms paralleled their endeavours between 1920 and 1930. Their first car, the side-valve 10/30 hp, was well thought of, but the pushrod overhead-valve development of it, the 12/50, won the 1923 Brooklands 200 Mile Race at 93.29 mph soon after its introduction, the only British car to achieve a 200 Mile Race win during the series. Although entirely conventional in design, the 12/50 was the most successful 1½-litre British sports car of its time, both commercially and in competitions. From 1925 Alvis concentrated on developing their 1½-litre front-wheel-drive design, first with supercharged sprint and racing cars, some built to the current Grand Prix formula, although lack of finance prevented their full development. Sports four-cylinder versions won their class in the Le Mans 24 Hour Race in 1928 at the first attempt, and one of these all-independently-sprung cars took second place in the 1928 TT.

The straight-eight twin-overhead-camshaft super-charged fwd sports cars gave a good account of themselves in the 1930 TT where they were runners-up to the Italian Alfa Romeos, and the engines of these Alvises, of which only a handful were produced, were indeed up to contemporary Alfa Romeo and Bugatti standards. The slump stopped further development of the very advanced fwd design after some 155 cars had been made, and Alvis concentrated on more conventional four- and six-cylinder cars. They were amongst the pioneers of independent suspension and synchromesh gearboxes on British production cars in the early 'thirties.

Triumph cars, associated with the motor-cycle firm, were first made in Coventry in 1923. The initial efforts in 10/20 and 13/30 form with side-valve four-cylinder engines, were not very distinguished, although the latter model in 1925 was the first British car to have Lockheed contracting-type hydraulic brakes. Their best seller was the 832 cc side-valve Super 7, with hydraulic brakes and worm final drive introduced in 1928, some examples of which were supercharged. It was never a threat to the Austin Seven, a supercharged example of which, of only 747 cc capacity and with side-valves, won the Brooklands 500 Mile Race on October 1930, at an average speed of 83.41 mph having lapped at 87 mph.

This is an impressive enough achievement on which to close an account of the Veteran and Vintage years a period during which, as Dr Lanchester might have observed, a good many minds had been changed, both within the motor industry and outside it.

*Above:* Guy's first postwar effort was this robust 2½ ton lorry, introduced after the factory was released from wartime armaments work.

The First World War had a dramatic effect on the growth of heavy motor transport. It all but spelled the end of the horse except for local delivery work and it trained thousands of drivers and mechanics in the intricacies of motor vehicles. Into this atmosphere were born two names that were later to play an important part in British Leyland. One was Guy, which had appeared briefly before the war with a 30-cwt model carrying such unusual features as an overdrive top gear and pressed-steel frame, and the other was Scammell. An example of a Guy that spent its life as a coal lorry in the Farnborough area can be seen at Donington.

The Scammell articulated seven-tonner was a milestone in heavy-goods' transport: it first appeared in prototype form in 1919 and entered production at Watford in 1921—22. Until that time most loads of over five tons had been handled by cumbersome steam vehicles. The Scammell, originally a seven-tonner that rapidly grew to ten tons', twelve tons'—and even greater—capacity, was a heavy-duty rigid four-wheeler to which was attached a partially super-imposed trailer. It was claimed to have the running costs of a three-tonner and was the first popular articulated vehicle in Britain. The idea was not new, having been first tried by Thornycroft in 1898.

Although Britain was extremely successful at making heavy commercial vehicles, the 15—30 cwt end of the market had been largely neglected by both the car makers and by the lorry and bus makers. This was because neither had surplus car components of the right size and most of the successful vehicles came from America and were so cheap that no British firm could afford to develop a competitor that would sell at a sufficiently low price.

A batch of Lanchester armoured vehicle chassis.

*Above:* Like the car from which it derived, the Bean 25 cwt was a well made design but could not survive against Morris Commercial opposition.

*Pictures on opposite page*

*Top*
An Aveling steam roller—the oldest in Britain—and a Leyland Lynx fire engine

*Centre left*
Scammell 100-ton articulated tractor of 1927 on a HCVC run to Brighton

*Centre right*
Leyland single-decker on a run to Brighton

*Bottom left*
1910 Austin outside a reconstruction of a typical period garage

*Bottom right*
A 1929 Austin Seven butcher's van still in use

*Above:* Originally set up by a bus operator to meet his own requirements, Bristol also built goods vehicles for other users.

*Left:* Built to meet the competition in the light goods field offered by USA makes, the one-ton Morris Commercial was to remain in production for 15 years and helped ensure the strength of the British industry.

Leyland decided to tackle this field in 1922 by adopting the Trojan car design and producing it in a former wartime armaments' factory at Kingston-on-Thames as both a car and light van. They were moderately successful, even if the unconventional design of the vehicle with its chain drive and two-stroke engine put off many prospective purchasers. Brooke Bond were not unhappy with it: their little red vans were a familiar sight for over thirty years. Leyland eventually sold its Trojan subsidiary and replaced it at Kingston in 1931 with the 30 cwt to 2-ton six-cylinder Cub range.

Two other manufacturers to look at the vast potential market for light commercial vehicles in the early 'twenties were Morris and Bean. Both had successfully broken into the market for mass-production cars and now sought to combat the Americans with vehicles using as high a proportion of existing car components as possible to keep down the price.

Both the Morris-Commercial Tonner and the Bean 25 cwt appeared in 1924 using 14-horsepower car engines made by the two arch-rivals. Both were very successful, though the Morris had the edge on price and by the end of 1930 had ousted the Bean and indeed many of its overseas competitors, The Morris-Commercial T, or Tonner, remained in production for roughly twenty years, as did its lighter L sister model. They were joined by a vast proliferation of other Morris-Commercials, in the early 'thirties: from light delivery vans up to double-deck buses. Without even including the light Morris-car-derived vans and pick-ups, they were Britain's largest commercial vehicle makers for many years; typical annual production in the 'twenties and 'thirties being around 10,000 vehicles.

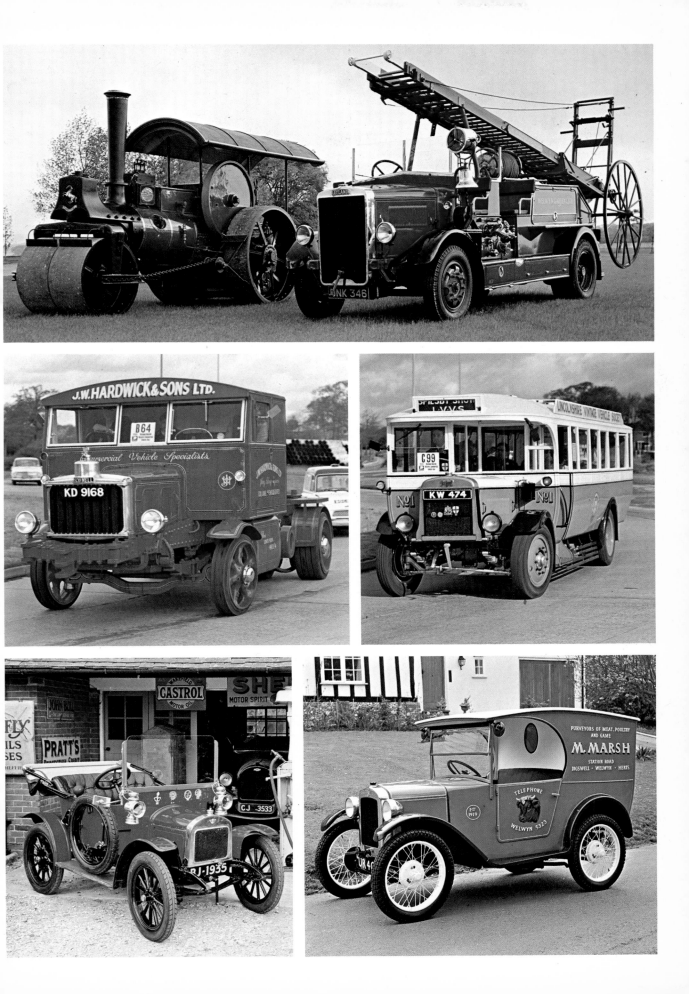

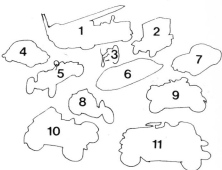

### From the Donington Collection

Some exhibits from the Leyland Historic Vehicles Ltd. Collection, which share the show halls at Donington Park with the cars of the Tom Wheatcroft Collection of racing cars.

1 the 1934 Leyland Lynx fire engine

2 the 1910 Austin Endcliffe landaulette

3 the 1876 Lever tricycle

4 the Morris Minor of 1948

5 the Thornycroft 4-cylinder car chassis

6 the 1939 Gardner-MG recordbreaker

7 the '100mph-for-seven-days' Jaguar XK 120 Coupe

8 the 1897 Wolseley

9 the 1906 Riley

10 the 8hp Rover

11 the original Bull-nose Morris of 1913

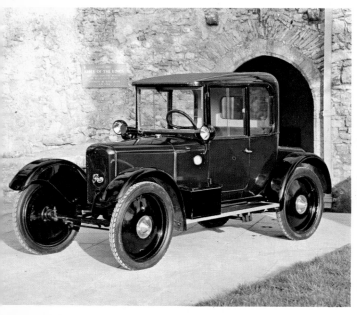

*Pictures on opposite page*

*Top left*
The Leyland steam lawnmower of 1899

*Top right*
1903 Triumph motor cycle

*Centre left*
The 1903 Wolseley designed by Herbert Austin

*Centre right:*
Riley Lynx in a Silverstone Vintage Sports-Car Club race

*Bottom left*
The 8hp flat-twin Rover in 'doctor's coupe' form, a cycle car of the early 'twenties

*Bottom right*
1937 Wolseley Super Six cabriolet, used by Lord Nuffield until his death in 1963

*Below:* By the end of the 'twenties, Maudslay had carved out a useful niche in the luxury coach field. With its built-in toilet facilities, this was probably intended for Continental touring.

*Above:* Established to build buses for a group of London operators, AEC were strong contenders throughout the 'twenties with vehicles such as this open-top double-decker.

Meanwhile, important developments were taking place in the passenger-transport world. Bristol, like AEC, originally a vehicle manufacturer set up by a local bus operator, had started selling two- and four-ton goods/passenger models to outside customers in the early 'twenties, and AEC had concentrated on replacing London's ageing B-type fleet. Initially the replacements had been forward control K-types followed by the S, but in 1923, with the NS, AEC became the first British manufacturer to offer a drop-frame bus. Until then most bus and coach chassis had been identical to goods models, except perhaps for a changed rear axle ratio for higher touring speeds and softer springs for passenger comfort. The NS did away with the straight frame and instead had a chassis built close to the road with a swept-up portion over each axle. The bus was easier to board and centre of gravity was lower—an important point on a double-decker, especially one that was intended to have an enclosed roof (on misguided safety grounds the roof was banned for two years).

The drop frame was taken a stage further in 1924, first by Maudslay and then by Leyland. The Maudslay was the first in a long line of special low-line safety charabanc and coach chassis that were to become a speciality of the Maudslay works in Coventry. The Leyland was even more important, being the legendary Lion, the first low-frame bus to achieve mass sales on the open market (the AEC was mainly confined to London for several years). Over 2,500 Lions had been sold by the end of 1928 and in the previous year they had been joined by the equally important six-cylinder 'low bridge' Titan double-decker and its Tiger single-deck sister. Albion and Guy quickly followed suit with specifically-designed passenger chassis, the latter adopting Daimler sleeve-valve six-cylinder engines in several examples. This engine was also used briefly by AEC following an unusual partnership between the two firms in 1927, during which their commercial vehicles were called ADC or Associated Daimler. ADC was primarily a central policy and sales headquarters that left the actual manufacture of vehicles to AEC at their

With its modern-type wellbase wheels and tyres and traditional char-a-banc body, this Daimler combined old and new.

new plant at Southall, and of certain components to Daimler. Though the fusion was short lived it created the new generation of Daimler passenger models, the first being the CF6, as well as the advanced light-weight AEC 423/4 and 426.

Just as the heavy lorries accepted by the War Department in the First World War had been made to a partially standardised design, so the War Office in the early 'twenties formulated plans for a vehicle to suit their future needs. Instead of the lumbering solid-tyred three-tonners of the 1914—18 period, the new vehicle emerged as a lively 30-cwt truck on pneumatic tyres with ample reserves of strength for working on or off the road. Several companies that are now in British Leyland produced examples but perhaps the two best remembered in civilian transport circles are the Albion SB24 and the Thornycroft A series. Born in 1923, these models and their successors were the backbone of many light goods' fleets in the 'twenties and 'thirties and could comfortably carry 2—3 tons on the road.

Thornycroft also made a speciality of heavier military and colonial trucks. They made the first British all-wheel-drive lorry, the four-four Hathi in 1924; a six-wheel-drive version was also experimented with. Scammell, too, took an interest in heavy off-road vehicles in 1927 with their six-four Pioneer, available

from 1929 with six-wheel drive. This model was to prove a formidable vehicle for opening up overseas oil fields and for extra-heavy civilian and military transport all over the world. It was joined in 1929 by an even vaster machine, the first 100-ton-capacity lorry in the world, a tractor and trailer combination, the tractor having Scammell's usual 80 bhp four-cylinder petrol engine driving by chain two short rear axles set end to end and each having two sets of double solid-tyred wheels.

As a natural continuation of the 30-cwt War Office theme a six-wheel 3-ton version was evolved in the mid-'twenties and Thornycroft, Guy, Crossley, Morris-Commercial, Albion, and Leyland became important suppliers of both military and civilian versions, many of which played an important transport role in the developing countries because of their ability to work off hard roads. Lanchester also made variations as the basis for armoured cars. AEC became involved with off-road vehicles when they acquired the British Four Wheel Drive Lorry Company in 1929, a firm that had originally reconditioned American army lorries but which had then built its own vehicles with an increasing number of AEC parts. These specialised vehicles were subsequently called AEC or Hardy and directly lead to the famous four × four Matador and six × six AEC of World War Two.

Semi-forward control for Leyland with tanke body of early 'thirties.

# 1930-1940 TOWARDS A MATURE INDUSTRY

*Above:* Pioneering move by Morris in 1933 was the traffic signal indicator, but it was shortlived. Expertise of Pressed Steel Company, which Morris helped set up in the mid-'twenties, shows in the body.

*Right:* A best seller, the Morris Eight of 1935 was available as saloon, tourer or van. It had a 918 cc side valve engine and a three-speed gearbox.

Throughout the 'twenties the manufacturers' ideas about how a car should be made changed little in Britain. The watercooled engine sat upright at the front of the chassis, and drove through a three- or four-speed gearbox to a rear axle equipped with half-elliptic springs. The front axle, too, was on half-elliptics and independent suspension was largely a theoretical possibility.

But the ideas of the customer were certainly changing. The four-seater open tourer with plastic sidescreens and a waterproof hood was his most popular choice in 1920; by 1930 the saloon car had taken the ascendancy it has held to this day. A desire by drivers and passengers for more comfort and convenience led to those cars that enjoyed a long production run putting on weight as bodies became more elaborate, larger brakes were added, and wheels and tyres became more bulky to cushion shocks from the road.

It was time for a change in 1930 and several years later the change was complete. Popular car design was by 1938 close to being drawn in the pattern it was to keep for nearly four decades. It needed a keen eye to see it at the time.

*Right:* Outwardly conventional, the 1939
Morris Ten-Four Series M was an early
example of chassis-less monocoque
body construction and was given
suspension anti-roll bars after
experiments by the young Alec
Issigonis.

*Left:* The Morris Eight Series E, with its
built-in headlamps, had a four-speed
gearbox and was to remain in
production until superseded by the
Minor of 1948.

In the popular field, William Morris had seen his medium size popular-car market shrink in months at the end of the 'twenties as the slump bit into the customer's pocket. The Morris Minor and its overhead-camshaft engine made little impact on the well-entrenched Austin Seven and even meticulously plotted promotions such as the 1931 exercise in which the newly introduced £100 side-valve Minor was persuaded to do 100 mpg and then later 100 mph at Brooklands, could do little to help. The Austin Seven went on its way, until even it became too portly for its own good and the Super Seven Forlite ended its long career early in 1939.

Meanwhile, after some fairly worrying years, Morris found a winner in the small-car stakes with the Morris Eight of 1934. Neat and snub-nosed, with a rubber-mounted side-valve engine, a syncromesh three-speed gearbox and hydraulic brakes, it was a winning combination. Backed by an extensive range of cars from Cowley and Longbridge, Austin and Morris between them accounted for close to 60 per cent of the popular market in Britain at that time. The Morris Eight grew up to become the Series E, still with the ex-Minor side-valve engine, but sporting a neat pressed-steel body with the chassis and body bolted together to provide semi-unitary construction. The final step to unitary construction came when the Morris Ten Series M appeared with a chassis-less monocoque body to house its lively overhead-valve engine. Front anti-roll bars were fitted to the benefit of roadholding. Lacking only independent front suspension to become a true prototype of the modern family saloon, the M-Series was a milestone. The Ten Four Morris of 1939 gave 38 bhp on 1100 cc.

Austin, too, although they were less enterprising than Morris in body construction, developed a useful

*Left:* Standard themselves moved forward in style with the Flying Standard saloons of 1936. This is the Twelve.

10 hp engine in 1934, using the newly introduced steel backed thin wall big end, which made possible great strides in engine performance from engines of modest specification.

As the 'thirties opened the Standard company moved towards mass production in the Nine, which slotted into the market just above Austin and the Morris. The basic chassis of the 16 and 21 hp Standards was a robust low-slung affair, and side-valve engines ranging from 1600 to 2660 cc gave them a lively performance. The 16 hp engine with seven main bearings was famed for its long life. The company, too, moved towards unitary construction with the Flying Standard range of 1936 in which the cruciform chassis was without side members and was attached to the body so that the body sills became part of the chassis.

The Standard V8 of the same period, an up-market foray, was followed by the Eight of 1938, a direct attack on the low-price market and with the attraction of a fine little four-cylinder overhead-valve engine and acceptable independent front suspension.

All benefited from Flying Standard coachwork styling, in which sweeping lines set off a careful finish. The range was highly successful and by the end of the 1930s the company was in a strong position.

The early 1930s were the day of the small six, and Triumph introduced its Scorpion for this market. This model, the Super Nine, used engines from Coventry Climax.

The Triumph-motor-cycle side of the business had continued parallel to the cars, providing a steady cash flow when the years of the slump made it increasingly difficult for companies such as Triumph to operate at a profitable sales level. But in 1930 the cycle connection was dropped from the company title and the two-

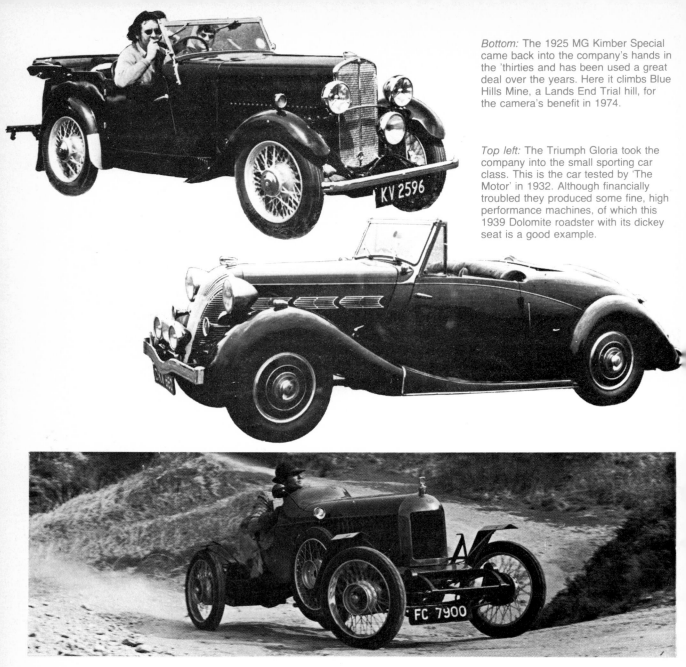

wheelers were sold off a few seasons later, to raise cash for new car production.

Handicapped by a shortage of cash for development and tooling, the Triumph Company was unable to build its own engines and went to Coventry Climax, specialist engine builders since 1917, who had a useful range of power plants. Apart from use as industrial engines, these units powered AJS, Crossley, and other cars. Their four-cylinder overhead inlet, side-exhaust-valve engine of 1108 cc was installed in the Southern Cross sports tourers, of pleasing appearance and keenly priced. In 1933 an underslung chassis was introduced to give company stylists more scope, and the new range of four- and six-cylinder Triumph Glorias appeared, aiming at the small luxury sporting market.

Since the always financially embarrassed Triumph Company could not afford to tool its own engines, it continued to use the Coventry Climax units until, step by step, they were able to take over manufacture themselves. The Triumph Gloria range was available in a collection of neat saloons of sporting pretension, although with their small engines and considerable weight, performance was occasionally less than might have been expected from their aggressive appearance. Eventually, by 1936—37, engine sizes had crept up to 1767 cc for the 14/60 Dolomite and to 1991 cc for the six-cylinder version. Triumphs did well in the 1934 Monte Carlo Rally, finishing third and doing well in the Alpine Trial, winning the Coupe des Alpes, the manufacturers' team prize, for the 1100 cc class and individual Coupe des Glaciers.

The company briefly developed the spectacular supercharged eight-cylinder Dolomite, a costly exercise against a background of deepening financial

*Above:* Even limited-production versions such as the C-type MG Midget were built on the production line at Abingdon.

*Above:* One car never meant for production was the 750 cc supercharged Q-type Midget sports racer. With its four-cylinder engine in a K3 chassis it lapped Brooklands at over 122 mph and experiences with the design at these speeds led to the all-independent suspension R-type Midget.

difficulty, and it was not surprising that this promising design was shelved early in its development. Just before the beginning of the war, the company announced a new Twelve, a quietly-styled four-cylinder car that would have taken them away from the market they had occupied for the previous years.

Although the MG Company was still remaindering off some of its fine 18/80 MG six-cylinder fast sports tourers as late as 1932, the company was firmly committed to the Midget series after its resounding victory in the 1930 Double Twelve Race at Brooklands. In those difficult days the little Midget was a brisk seller, and when in 1932 the J2 Midget with its slab tank and long swept wings appeared the company was set for enormous success.

The Midgets rapidly went through the letters of the alphabet as they were improved and developed. The 939 cc PB was the last of the overhead-camshaft Midgets with an engine evolved from the original Morris Minor, and it was followed by the TA and then the TB, with the pushrod overhead-valve engine of the Morris Ten. These later Midgets, as so often happened with new models from this marque, were compared unfavourably with their predecessors, but went on to create an enormous new market for themselves. The statistics speak for themselves: 2,000 of the M-type, 20,000 of the T-type were built.

It was in these years that there was the first full development of the idea that production, engines, gearboxes, axles, even chassis, originally intended for quite mundane cars, could be successfully adopted by a sports car manufacturer. For the first time, too, a full range of tuning equipment was available to take an enthusiastic owner stage by stage to what he could

*Below:* Long distance racing at Brooklands forced the pace of MG development. The Magic Midget (8) and Horton's MG (11) could lap at over 104 mph.

*Above:* Track-racing version of the K3 MG used by George Eyston. It was later to be evolved into the 203 mph plus Gardner—MG illustrated in the colour spread.

afford—even to full international racing level.

The MG factory also produced a comprehensive range of other sporting cars as well as the Midget. Some sold briskly, some did not. Some part of the success of the Midgets must be attributed to international racing successes by the various racing cars derived from production MGs. The 1931 C-type Monthlery Midget was the first of these and MG's racing programme culminated in the magnificence of the 1100 cc K3 Magnette, now considered to be one of the outstanding sports racing cars of all time. If continental racing designers had led in the evolution of the classic racing car with its long flexible chassis, short stiff half-elliptic road-springs, non-independent suspension front and rear and highly supercharged powerplant, it was the Abingdon factory that took it to its finest expression.

The K3 raced and won, and when MG gave up its works' racing programme in 1935, one was re-bodied and re-developed into a straight-line record-breaker to take International class records at speeds up to 203.5 av. mph for the flying kilometre on the Dessau Autobahn in Germany, a performance that, some forty years later, has not been surpassed by any other 1100 cc class car.

MG was aware that if they were to continue to progress at the same pace, a new approach to design for roadholding was imperative; by 1935 they had the R-type racing Midget with full independent suspension and backbone chassis. Much later a production MG was to benefit from the work on the R-type.

It was ironic that although the Minor was never able to dislodge the Austin Seven, the Minor's descendant the Midget, was usually much more than a match for

High 'thirties styling. The costly, handbuilt Vanden Plas bodied Alvis *above* has a finely judged dual colour scheme involving different colours for the wheels. The Riley Kestrel makes good use of the traditional Riley diamond symbol in window and bonnet louvre outlines.

the Austin, when as in the case of the C-type, they were racing in the same class. To counter this opposition, Herbert Austin authorised a series of little racing single-seaters, based on the Seven but with exceptionally highly developed supercharged engines. Endowed with narrow high-tailed bodies not unlike those of American dirt track racers, the 750 cc racers were at last a match for the Midgets, when redesigned and fitted with exquisite little twin-overhead-camshaft engines in 1936, they were truly formidable.

Mainstay of Riley's production in the period was the Nine with its ingenious high-camshaft ohv hemispherical cylinder head. It tended to put on weight as time passed but remained a graceful and appealing small car in such carefully finished versions as the four-light 9 hp Kestrel of 1935 and the later Kestrel Sprite. Riley, too, was a major racing marque, and the famous White Riley developed by **Raymond** Mays and Peter Berthon from the elegant six-cylinder MPH two-seater sports led to the racing ERAs which made a great impact on the small car racing scene of 1934.

Freddie Dixon, with his multi-carburetted racing Rileys, was an early exponent of modern methods of tuning unsupercharged engines. The company made commercial capital of the racing successes with the Sprite and Imp two-seater sports models and the Lynx four-seater fast tourers. Riley were keen users of the

epicyclic preselector gearbox, which, with a centrifugal clutch, much simplified driving.

They had the misfortune to be caught in the recession of the late 'thirties, and after abortive talks with the equally hard-pressed Triumph management, were bought by Lord Nuffield in 1938. Production continued with simplified four-cylinder models, a four-door saloon, and a drophead two-door.

Not all specialised manufacturers found themselves in such difficulties. Alvis made a magnificent recovery after the public's indifference to the merits of their front-wheel drive cars brought them to the brink of disaster. They hurriedly put back into production an updated version of the four-cylinder 1500 cc 12/50 that had stood them in good stead for so long in the previous decade. At the same time, they put in hand a newer series of cars using a most attractive six-cylinder engine first seen as the 14.75 hp in the late 1920s.

In due course they led to the high performance 2½ litre Speed Twenty of 1931, which soon had a well-thought-out form of leaf-spring single-wishbone independent front suspension and which pioneered the use of the easy-to-use syncromesh gearbox in British cars. Never a cheap car, the Alvis was endowed with fine coachwork by traditional coachbuilders such as Cross and Ellis, or Vanden Plas. A simpler four-cylinder 12/70 was introduced in 1937, but by this time

the company was deeply involved with military fighting vehicles and aero engine developments, a decision taken in 1934, when it was realised that dependence on the difficult luxury car market could lead to disaster.

In the 1930s London was the home of many great coachbuilding houses. Hooper was renowned for superbly handcrafted, luxurious bodies on chassis of the highest quality, such as Daimler. Proudly they displayed the Royal warrant, and the Daimler—Hooper connection was symbolised by the sleeve-valve black limousines that swept silently, and bearing no number plates, out of the gates of Buckingham Palace.

Another house was Vanden Plas, originally of Belgium. Brought to England before the First World War to pioneer the design of the classic Torpedo open four-seater light touring body, they went on to produce possibly the finest sports touring bodies of the 'twenties on Bentley chassis and in the 'thirties built superb luxury bodies for Alvis, Lanchester, Daimler, and others. Their particular strength was the sweeping line of the high-quality, high-performance car.

Daimler entered the 'thirties building the lofty, silent, sleeve-valve engined formal cars for which they were renowned but had under their wing other makes such as BSA—named after the group's parent company— and Lanchester. In an early spate of badge engineering, Daimler used these names to try to exploit sections of the market new to them. There was a small-engined 10 hp BSA family saloon and the clever, inexpensive, little Scout front-wheel drive three- and four-wheelers were popular through the middle to late 'thirties. Lanchester was used as a name for a middle price 15/88 hp model, although there was a straight-eight chassis that could be endowed with luxury formal coachwork and was popular with members of royalty at home and overseas.

Daimler production policy was highly tortuous in the 1930s and offered a variety of designs from the sleeve-valve 12 cylinder Double Six up to 1937 to the 4.6 litre eight-cylinder of 1935, but a most important development was the pushrod ohv six-cylinder 2½ litre type of 1938. This was in no way a chauffeur's car, and with its

combination of smooth power and preselector gearbox with fluid flywheel, first introduced in 1931, offered a real step forward in easy driving and high performance in the luxury medium-size car. It was truly a modern design and was to be extensively developed, gaining coil spring independent front suspension on the way through into the post-war period after 1945.

Another company to hit the jackpot with a design that carried them through into the 1940s was the beleaguered Rover, after thrashing about with some fairly disastrous changes of policy, including an attack on the cheap end of the market with the 10/25 Family Ten in 1930—31. But in 1933 there was a change of policy with a new management who brought out a continental-type Hastings Coupe on the 10 hp chassis in 1933. With a similar range of saloons, long-bonnetted, close-coupled, notably well equipped and finished, the Rovers came on strongly in the 1930s. By 1939 the 10 and 12 hp versions were fours, the 14, 16, and 20 hp were sixes, all with transmission freewheels.

New policy at Rover under S. B. Wilks is illustrated by 1936 14 hp Rover four-door saloon.

Perhaps one other maker in its class could match the line of the 1936 SS Jaguar 2½ litre tourer.

Continental in feeling, the SS I remained in production from 1933 to 1936.

No motor industry can survive without the support of the host of specialists providing components and services. Companies such as ENV were specialists in rear axles and gearboxes, supplying many car companies. They evolved their own rugged and reliable epicyclic preselector gearboxes. One manufacturer of high performance cars in southern England found the ENV gearboxes it used were so reliable that it was unnecessary to carry a spares inventory.

Another fringe company was Henry Meadows, established in 1919. Their engines were used in the thirties by high-performance car builders like Lagonda as well as by truck manufacturers and found their way into industrial applications such as electrical generators and fire pumps, just like the rather smaller efforts of Coventry Climax.

The 'twenties were a period in which a car had a particular role to play. If it was a family car then it was customarily spacious but ponderous and slow-moving, a baby car then tiny, cramped and uncertain in brakes and steering. Luxury cars were precisely that and habitually expensive. Sports cars if small were noisy, spartan, inclined to temperament, if large,

thirsty, costly to purchase, and potentially ruinous to maintain. In the 'thirties things began to change. More makers began to follow the lead established by the MG models derived from Morris, in which a whole range of designs to suit different tastes and uses could be evolved from one basic set of components. The Morris Isis Six powerplant could be used for ordinary touring cars, in the MG 18/80 Six guise, and was basically medium-price Wolseley.

But the most striking example of this principle was that of the SS. Derived from the underslung chassis Standards, the SS1 of 1931, introduced to the public after a series of tantalising advertisements, was a highly glamorous package, offering remarkable value for money. The SS soon developed into a range of luxurious sporting cars of considerable refinement. They were regarded with the gravest suspicion by the motoring experts, for it seemed impossible that so much style, and with the later side-valve SS 90 and overhead-valve 100 sports models, such high performance, could be available at such a price. But William Lyons had got his sums right; by avoiding overlapping models that competed against themselves, by aggres-

sive and appealing advertising, he swiftly carved a lasting place in the market for his products.

An important development, seen in the SS Jaguar saloons of 1937, was the move away from traditional wooden-framed metal-panelled body construction, to all-steel methods of flow-line production, more or less unheard of development in this slice of the market. Output boosted, he was able to improve specification and equipment without price increases, and it was hardly surprising that his competitors were in one kind of trouble or another in the late 'thirties.

*Top:* The SS Jaguar 100, in production as a 2½ litre from 1935 to 1939 and as a 3½ litre from 1937 to 1939, was loved or hated by enthusiasts but is now one of the great classics. It is pictured outside the old Foleshill, Coventry, main entrance of the factory.

*Bottom:* The essence of prewar motor sport. 1938 SS100 on the Scottish Rally, Loch Tay in background.

# COMMERCIAL VEHICLES

*Above:* With the diesel powered AEC Mammoth Major Eight of the mid-'thirties, road transport moved into the modern, multi-axled, high-speed era. Many, like the later example shown, were exported.

*Right:* Morris Commercial kept up the pressure through the 'thirties with a light range suitable for many uses and all powered by petrol engines.

1930 was the year AEC entered the goods' transport world in full force with their advanced Mercury, Monarch, Majestic, and Mammoth models. Some could be fitted with AEC's own diesel engine, which had been running since 1928 in prototype form and which in 1929 had made AEC the first British manufacturer to make a complete diesel vehicle themselves, as opposed to buying an engine from an outside supplier. This diesel vehicle was a bus and from 1930 AEC supplied production diesel buses to the London General Omnibus Company, who for many years were the largest single users of diesels in the world. In 1932 the highly advanced Q-type bus appeared with side-mounted engine and pre-selective gearbox. Leyland introduced a Gearless Tiger bus in 1933 and a year later could claim that almost half of Britain's diesel buses were Leyland engined. In 1933 AEC became an entirely independent company, though still with a contract to supply London with 90 per cent of its bus requirements and in 1934 they introduced the first internal-combustion-engined rigid eight-wheeler, the immortal Mammoth Major 8.

HTF 574

Leyland had introduced their famous animal-name goods' range in 1929, Beaver, Bison, Buffalo, Bull, Hippo, and from 1934, the Octopus eight-wheeler. They soon had their own successful diesel engine which, with vast exports of trucks and buses around the world, soon helped to oust the petrol engine from heavy vehicles. Leyland were successful, too, with fire engines, having offered special chassis since 1910; and in 1935 they produced the largest escape of the time—the 150 ft Leyland Metz. Albion and Thornycroft soon had their own diesels and offered equally wide ranges of vehicles. To gain room for expansion in 1935

*Top:* Leyland attacked the mass production builders in the light class with the Cub, seen in heavier six-wheel form. They offered both petrol and oil engines through the period.

*Centre:* The Crossley Condor double-decker was available with six-cylinder oil engine.

*Bottom:* Thornycroft's Sturdy of 1935 had a long career as a four- and five-ton commercial and was well suited to forward control van bodies.

Albion took over the factory of former Scottish rivals, Halley. Guy continued to concentrate on medium-weight trucks, took over their old neighbours Star in 1927, and eventually ended Star commercial-vehicle production in 1932. The well known Guy Wolf two-tonner appeared in 1933, followed by the 3/4 ton Vixen in 1934 and the 4½ ton Otter in 1935. These largely gave way in 1936 to a military design called the Ant, which used many common components from the ordinary haulage range including the Meadows engine. Meadows were important suppliers of proprietary engines to many vehicle manufacturers and they were eventually acquired by Jaguar along with Guy in the 1960s. Another important maker of proprietary engines especially for high-speed coaches, in the early 'thirties

*Above:* Leyland's military products were no beauties but the knowledge provided by worldwide operations under tremendous pressure was to be invaluable in the hard postwar world.

*Below:* Thornycroft continued to build semi-trailers such as the Strenuous, while the Sturdy too was available as a tractive unit.

was Coventry Climax, who also joined Jaguar in 1964.

Maudslay hit the headlines in 1934 with the first legal-length single-deck bus/coach able to carry forty passengers in comfort. This SF40, later called the Magna, and its more conventional sister, the Marathon, kept Maudslay occupied until they re-entered the heavy goods vehicle market in 1939. Meanwhile Leyland had produced their own example amongst the first all-steel bus bodies in 1934, and in 1937 they were one of the first companies to try a six-wheeler with two steering front axles. This emerged as the popular Steer goods' model and Gnu passenger chassis.

Morris-Commercial had very successfully increased their share of the mass-produced light- and medium-weight market in the 'thirties with the T and L and with the Transatlantically-styled C range, from 30 cwt to 4 tons in 1935, which was followed by the CV or Equiload —30 cwt to 5 tons— in 1937. The name Equiload was chosen because the set-back front put a similar weight on each tyre when the vehicle was laden, which helped tyre life and braking.

In 1939 Austin re-entered the medium-truck market after fifteen years in which they had only offered car-based commercial vehicles, notably vans and ambulances. These 30 cwt—3 ton Austins were soon produced in enormous quantities for the war effort, where they were joined by tens of thousands of Morris-Commercials, Guys, Leylands, AECs, Scammells, Thornycrofts, Albions, Crossleys RAF tractors, and Maudslays. The war years brought important developments in technology. Guy, for instance, discovered how to weld armour-plate steel, an important production improvement.

When the Second World War ended there was an enormous worldwide demand for commercial vehicles but there were serious material shortages, with steel allocated to vehicle manufacturers on the basis of their export record.

When production began to get under way again in 1945—46, the industry had already begun the moves to group together that were to lead to British Leyland. The Nuffield Organisation covered Morris, MG, Wolseley, and Riley, and it was matched in size by Austin, who undertook an enormous expansion programme in the postwar years. Standard had bought Triumph, and under the BSA panoply were Daimler and Lanchester. Sturdily independent were Jaguar, Rover, and Alvis.

Riley were quick off the mark in 1945 with the re-styled four-cylinder 1½ litre, its fabric-covered roof and sweeping lines evolved after intimate study of immediate prewar German practice. Rover, too, were early back in the market with basically prewar designs. In the popular market the unitary Morris Ten and the near-unitary Morris 8 Series E continued. Austin, using a punt-shaped chassis to which the body structure was bolted, embarked on the first stages of development of its 1200 cc engine that was to lead to the celebrated BMC B-series unit.

*Above:* One of the first makers to announce its postwar range was Riley, who later offered the rare drophead coupe as well as saloons.

*Below:* Alec Issigonis's original Minor, with low set headlamps and waffle-toaster grille. It remained for over 20 years.

Jaguar continued as before, but with saloons only in 1½, 2½ and 3½ litre form and dropped the SS 100, in anticipation of a new sporting model a couple of seasons later. Alvis had a pleasing development of the prewar 12/70 in the four-cylinder Fourteen, available, too, only as a saloon at first.

But the industry was set for a big step forward three years later. Designs for a new generation of small cars were well under way at Morris, Austin, and Standard. Greatest of these was Alec Issigonis's Morris Minor, introduced at the first postwar motor show in 1948. Initially equipped with the ex-Morris Eight side-valve powerplant but with torsion bar front suspension, rack and pinion steering, and the spacious body shell it was to keep for twenty-one years of production: the Minor was a small landmark. Unlike their competitors, Austin's new generation, the A40 Devon, the A70, retained separate chassis and body structures. But there was independent front suspension plus a good range of four-cylinder engines to which some fine gearboxes were coupled. It was to the A40 Devon of 1952 that the first 1200 cc version of the famous B-series engine was fitted.

The unitary construction Standard Eight and Ten used a development of the prewar ohv Eight engine and this, too, was to remain in production for another couple of generations. In response to what was seen as a pressing need to produce a medium-sized car for world markets, Standard introduced the bulky Vanguard 2 litre saloon, which had a heavy four-cylinder engine first seen in Ferguson tractors made by the company and which was to have a considerable competition future.

Triumph, faced with production problems of lack of pressed steel facilities and of materials, launched a line of appealing cars in the 1800 saloon (later the Renown) and Roadster, initially both using Standard-based four-cylinder engines. They plumped for a tubular chassis and a body of aluminium, that of the Renown being a classically-conceived hard-edged design of considerable aesthetic merit.

Jaguar produced its new Mark V saloon before the 1948 London Show. But along with the Minor, the great sensation of the Show was the new Jaguar XK 120 roadster with its soon-to-be-legendary twin-overhead-camshaft 120 bhp powerplant and its voluptuously modern outline. The magnificent engine introduced sporting motorists to an entirely new performance experience and took the Jaguar at one leap far beyond any competitor within many thousands of pounds of its price.

Exports were the cry of the day, and the Nuffield Organisation was gratified to discover that its TC MG Midget was in strong demand with a whole new generation of sportscar-minded motorists in the USA. It was an example of what might be considered to be an essentially obsolete design finding a new lease of life. Successive Midgets, the TD with its independent front suspension and 1500 cc engine and the TF, with its revised front-end treatment with built-in headlights, sold briskly overseas. During the four years from 1948 to the end of 1952 the British motor industry moved towards the type of product and the organisation it has today. Bulk of production was of light, simple family cars available in a variety of degrees of equipment and finish and for the most part with overhead-valve engines. Front suspension was independent, while that at the rear was still leaf spring. Hydraulic drum brakes were the preferred system, though some more conservative makers such as Rover retained the mechanical brakes that had given good service over the years for a season or two yet.

With Rover, priced above the popular saloons, were Triumph and Riley, once again with conventional chassis frames and separate body structures. Rover moved gently towards unitary construction in the chassis of the 60 and 75 of 1948. The frame supported the engine and gearbox and suspension as a unit but was cut short halfway back towards the gearbox rear axle. Full unit construction came in 1949 with the

*Right:* The Rover 60 and 75 models of 1948 were slightly updated versions of prewar saloons.

*Left:* The Austin A135 Princess was bodied by Vanden Plas, and now the factory builds Daimler Double Twelve limousines with other Jaguar/Daimler variants.

full-width body of the P4 series. In the following year they introduced their first turbine car and this mobile laboratory was the first of a series that was to culminate in the high-performance Rover—BRM turbine that raced at Le Mans in 1963 and 1965. A third layer was represented by the slightly more expensive Alvis, the Fourteen superseded in 1950 by the 3 litre of similar concept and available as a particularly fine drophead version, which in twin-carburettor Grey Lady form was a 90 mph+ vehicle.

Daimler, in the 1950s. was inclined to make press headlines at London Show-time, at the behest of the colourful Docker family, who ran the company, with a series of unconventionally-styled showpiece bodies by Hooper or Baker on the 5½ Straight Eight. In the background and providing a solidly profitable basis for such extravagances were the DB 18 Daimlers, the Conquest Century, the special sports coupe by Barker, and others.

Not overweight by contemporary standards and able in the Production races that were now a popular part of big international meetings at Silverstone, Goodwood

and other circuits to show a clean pair of heels to other nominally more sporting designs, the Daimlers were an entirely charming combination of conservative good manners and quality finish.

In 1952 low-price sports-car development took an important step forward with the introduction of the Triumph TR, Standard Vanguard-engined, seen at Earls Court in prototype form, and the Austin-Healey Hundred. Sports cars pretty and sports car plain, they took up the now well-established philosophy of using standard mechanical components in light windcheating body shells. Donald Healey's Hundred used the rugged and simple Austin A90 engine and running gear and initially possessed a windscreen arranged to fold flat by slipping along a track on the top of the body scuttle.

New high-speed capabilities in this generation of sports cars were recognised by setting the occupants well down in the shell: as in the Jaguar XK 120 the driver sat in, rather than on, his car.

But, more important for the future, the Nuffield and Austin concerns saw little point in continuing to

50

*Right:* The plain and simple TR series were to establish themselves as amongst the greatest of all sporting cars. This is a 1955/56 TR2.

*Above:* Works C-type Jaguar driven by Rolt at the 1953 Le Mans event.

*Right:* The Minor grew up to be the 1000 when the 1 litre BMC A-series engine was installed.

compete against each other with overlapping ranges and duplication of research and development facilities. It made a good deal of sense to come together and so in 1952 the British Motor Corporation was born. The jigsaw did not fit absolutely precisely. There was, for instance, the Austin A30 and the Morris Minor. The one with an acceptable body but an outstanding engine and gearbox, the other with outstanding body shell and suspension but with a stopgap engine installed while a suitable unit was tooled. The natural solution—the Minor 1000 using the A-series engine from Longbridge—was duly born in 1956. The A30 simultaneously grew to A35 and eventually slipped gracefully away in 1958. It was the same with the Morris Oxford, Cowley, and Wolseley models, which carried on through the fifties in counterpoint to their Longbridge counterparts, such as the Austin A50 Cambridge and the handsome A95 Westminster six-cylinder. A new generation of MG sports cars came along with the MGA in 1955. The B-series engine was installed in a neat full-width body equipped with conventional independent front and beam rear suspension, and the MGA made its debut as

a team of three entered for the Le Mans 24-Hours race. Its light structure endowed the car with an excellent performance from a simple 1500 cc pushrod ohv engine. The unit showed itself capable of substantial development as the MGA and its successor the MGB grew up, first to 1600 cc, then to 1800 cc. The B-series engine has now powered the MG sports models for more than two decades.

By 1957 the British motor industry had recovered from the trauma of the Suez debacle and was still the world's greatest exporter of motor vehicles. The B-series engine was put to use in the Wolseley 1500, a luxury small car larger than the Minor 1000, which, not surprisingly, turned out to have an exceptional performance. As late as this Austin were still using a combined body and chassis with long side members running the length of the body in the last chapter of the separate body and chassis story. The Austin Princess, the company's luxury flagship with its Vanden Plas coachbuilt body, was by the same year equipped with power steering and an automatic gearbox.

The biggest problem facing British stylists was to

51

come to terms with the full-width body. The coach-building companies were little help, for their early slab-sided postwar efforts were uniformly distressing, and an attempt by Hooper to evolve its own characteristic English line resulted in an uneasy compromise solution retaining elements of prewar ideas. Triumph tried to translate the architectural simplicity of the Renown into the slab-sided Mayflower, a small car using the Standard Eight engine, but the result was quaint indeed.

Finally, during 1957 and 1958 an approach to Pininfarina was made. This designer was at his tailfin period, but provided two well-balanced treatments. One was a three-box concept with the engine living in the first box, the occupants in the second larger box, with the luggage in the third smaller box behind. It resulted in the Austin A55/60 Cambridge, Morris Oxford, and Cowley and Wolseley 16/60. After an initial imbalance between body dimensions and wheel track had been sorted out, these were useful and attractive cars. The largest version, with a different body shell, was the later Austin A110 Westminster, of which there was subsequently a short-lived Rolls Royce-engined variant, the Princess R. This latter was possibly the best-looking of all the British Motor Corporation's production designs to that time, with its tailfins reduced to a minimum and neatly detailed general treatment.

In 1954 the Riley company, now building its cars at Abingdon, phased out the long-bonnetted Riley RME series and replaced it with the Pathfinder, which had its own unitary body shell, shared with the Wolseley 6/90. There were coil springs and radius arms to locate the rear axle. The old high-camshaft four-cylinder engine lived on until 1957, when it was replaced by a BMC variant with twin carburettors.

# COMMERCIAL VEHICLES

*Left:* Plain and practical—the military specification Maudslay Militant of 1939 to 1946, used in its thousands.

*Right:* Leyland trolleybuses served many cities. Equipped with Leyland own metal framed body, this example went to work in London.

AEC soon decided that the best future for the British heavy-vehicle industry lay in larger production units able to win orders of any size at competitive prices around the world. They took over Maudslay and Crossley in 1948 to create Associated Commercial Vehicles Ltd. Crossley were by now solely bus makers and Maudslay had become a major supplier of heavy goods' models, most of which had used AEC engines since the early days of the war.

Leyland soon followed suit by acquiring Albion and Scammell. In 1945 Guy acquired Sunbeam Trolley-buses, a descendent of the commercial vehicle side of the Sunbeam car firm that had made a few petrol-engined buses and coaches around 1930 but had then found its niche with electric vehicles. By coincidence Sidney Guy had worked at Sunbeam before founding Guy Motors, which helps to show just how intertwined the story of the various British motor companies is. Guy

*Right:* 'Feathers in our cap' slogan and a Red Indian mascot for the Guy Wolf which saw production through the 'thirties and the 'forties.

*Left:* The Scammell Mechanical Horse idea dates from 1933 and they found a thousand uses — such as this Service fire engine — before legislation ended their days.

*Below:* Introduced as a postwar stop-gap, the Land-Rover has passed the millionth built. The military can have their own lightweight version, suitable for parachute airdrop.

had been an important trolleybus maker, claiming the first pneumatic-tyred six-wheeler in 1926. Leyland and AEC pooled their trolleybus interests in a joint company in 1946 named BUT Ltd.

A major development in 1948 was the arrival of the go-anywhere Land-Rover from Rovers, who were anxious to break into the export field. A million Land-Rovers later this has proved to have been one of the most successful steps taken by the motor industry.

*Right:* Underfloor engined coaches such as this Leyland Royal Tiger ousted vertical engined vehicles in the late 1940s.

*Below:* Leyland's Comet, designed to appeal to world markets, first appeared in 1947.

*Left:* The Militant, a four wheel drive, six wheel military general service truck by ACV, demonstrates the complexity and high engineering standards to be found in this area.

One of the first entirely new post-war truck designs was the Leyland Comet of 1947, primarily intended for export. It was soon joined by many other famous foreign currency earners, such as the integral Olympic bus in 1950 and the Royal Tiger Worldmaster in 1954.

For British use, AEC introduced the Regal IV underfloor-engined bus in 1949, joined by the Reliance in 1954. Park Royal Vehicles, by now an ACV subsidiary, produced an integral version of this called the Mono-coach, which gave them valuable chassis-less construction experience when AEC introduced the next generation of vehicles for London Transport and other major operators.

# 1956-1976 THE CLASSIC DECADES

The XK engine of Heynes and Hassan and a body styled by Lyons, were brilliantly combined in the Jaguar Mk VII of 1950.

To match the fast saloons coming onto the market, with their improved brakes, steering and roadholding, production car races at circuits all over Britain took in cars like the Jaguar Mark VII, Daimler Conquest Century, MGZA Magnette, and Austins from the A35 to the big A105. In international rallying the 'fifties were a classic era and the BMC works team, set up in 1954, hit the headlines in event after event. Their MGAs and MGBs, Austin Healeys, large and small, and finally the Minis after their introduction in 1959, set standards other teams tried to beat. Development could be intensive. The big six-cylinder rally Austin Healey was finally equipped with costly chassis modifications and special engines with light alloy heads and blocks. The tough, economical Triumph TR sports series represented a pinnacle for every aspiring rallyman. Forerunner of the current MG Midget two-seater, the Austin Healey Sprite made a spectacular debut, coming first, second and third in its class in the 1958 Alpine Trial.

Pininfarina was also called on to draw up the Austin A40. Based on the existing components, the type was first seen at the Paris Motor Show in 1958. The neat A40 anticipated modern 'hatchback' styling with its wide third door at the rear giving access to the luggage space.

In Spring 1958, the Austin-Healey Sprite had appeared and took the British Motor Corporation back into small sports cars. Its 948 cc engine was the smallest sports-car engine they had used since MG's PB of the 'thirties. A lightweight shell with the characteristic 'frog-eyes' used a combination of A35 and Minor parts with quarter elliptic rear suspension. The end result was a highly manoeuvrable, entertaining car capable of a lively performance without overstressing its tiny engine.

During the mid 'fifties an MG speciality was class and championship victories by private owners. A

*Left:* The Rover—BRM which successfully competed at Le Mans in 1963 and 1965.

*Below:* An MGB wins the Marathon de la Route 1966; at 5,620 miles, the world's longest motor race.

private owner took the UK Championship for series-production sports cars in 1956. There were privateer victories at Sebring 12-Hours race in 1956 and 1957 and another took the 2-litres class at Le Mans in 1960 with his own fastback MGA.

But all must pale beside the achievement of the Jaguar. The first immediate postwar Alpine Trial victory with a revived prewar SS Jaguar 100 was a curtain-raiser. The arrival of the XK 120 opened the way to the Le Mans victories of the C and D type sports racers, which began in 1951 and culminated in the crushing 1957 result, when privately owned D types filled first, second, third, fourth, and sixth places.

The same engine went into the sumptuously appointed Jaguar Mk VII and this too showed its mettle, winning the Monte Carlo Rally two seasons after it was introduced in 1950.

The 'fifties were a period of epic struggles between works teams in the great long-distance rallies.

Triumph, operating with largely standard but carefully prepared TRs, became formidable adversaries to the BMC Competition Department. 1961 was a great year for the classic sports two-seaters and the big Austin-Healeys took five class victories in the classic events.

The introduction of the Mini in 1959 was to mark a revolution in small-car design. With its transverse engine, front wheel drive, rubber suspension and tiny body, which somehow found ample space for four substantial adults, it offered a combination of virtues previously thought totally unobtainable.

It took its class in the Geneva Rally of 1960 and to their delight the performance experts found they had a little cheap saloon that could be made to cover the ground as well as any thoroughbred sports car. The solid little A series engine became the focus of even greater attention than before. The Mini was not merely a class winner—it was a classic winner. In 1964 it won the Monte Carlo Rally and the following season the

*Below:* The Mini, introduced in 1959, opened a new chapter in small car design.

*Bottom:* Built in the light of the Le Mans victories the E-type Jaguar took sports cars into a new classic period in the 'sixties.

*Below:* With its clever 16-valve head, the Triumph Dolomite Sprint is a championship winner.

Mini-Cooper won fourteen international rallies.

The TR3 won the Manufacturers team prize at Le Mans in 1961 and the TR4 became a major rally campaigner. It was backed by the little Triumph Spitfire, which used a derivative of the long-lived Standard Eight engine. It marked up a class victory at Le Mans and recorded a remarkable sequence of successes in sports-car racing in the USA. The Midgets built up an impressive list of victories in the great international events. Coventry Climax produced the Grand Prix V8 engine which powered Jim Clark to the World Championship in 1963 and 1965.

During the past fifteen years some classic cars have emerged from British factories. The front-wheel drive transverse-engined concept has proved capable of enormous development and landmarks include the Hydrolastic-suspended BMC 1100—for years UK best-seller—and the aerodynamic Princess range. Rover won much praise for the thoughtful design of their 2000 saloon when it was introduced in 1963.

The idea of a powerful structure encapsulating the car's occupants is being developed in safety car research. In the safety-vehicle field, the Marina-based RSV2 showed that a car equipped with every design feature and safety device could still be an enjoyable to drive and a responsive machine.

Jaguar progressed with a range of increasingly luxurious and powerful machines. Their great achievement is the V12 engine, seen in the world-beating E-type Jaguar and the XJS and shortly to embark on a new international racing programme. MG and Triumph sports cars are now supplemented by the Triumph Dolomite with its elegant and efficient 16-valve Sprint engine, a racing championship winner.

The rear-engined Daimler Fleetline revealed new thinking about city bus design.

A new generation of goods models appeared from AEC, of which the Mercury of 1953 was the first to have the familiar stylish AEC cab, which remained in use until it was replaced by Leyland's Ergomatic design of 1964. Albion introduced their ingenious 4-ton-capacity underfloor-engined Claymore distribution model in 1955 and continued to make rugged reliable haulage and tipping chassis using an increasing proportion of Leyland components. Though the name Albion disappeared in 1972 many of their traditional model names live on with today's Scottish-built Leyland range.

In 1958 Leyland's Atlantean double-deck bus with transverse rear-mounted engine entered production after six years of development. It eventually replaced the more conventional Titan and was joined by the Daimler Fleetline. For a time a competitor was the equally revolutionary Guy Wulfrunian, which had disc brakes and air suspension and was a sister model to the familiar Arab. Guy's BMC-, AEC-, and Leyland-powered goods' range was replaced in 1964 by the very successful Big J series following Jaguar's 1961 takeover.

Crossley and Maudslay names disappeared from vehicles in the mid 'fifties and Thornycroft became increasingly specialised, producing such vehicles as the Nubian cross-country fire appliance chassis and the Mighty Antar heavy-haulage tractor. The Mighty Antar had first appeared in 1950 powered by a 250 bhp Rover Meteorite tank engine and eventually around a thousand of these gigantic vehicles, amongst the largest in the world, were in use.

Scammell, too, continued to build giant vehicles, which grew from the six-six Constructor of 1952 to today's vast Super Constructor tractors able to haul loads of several hundred tons. Scammell also remain-

ed important suppliers of more conventional goods'
vehicles as well as of their mechanical horses. These
familiar three-wheeled tractors had first appeared in
1933 as replacements for railway-company horses on
local deliveries from the station. In 1948 they had been
redesigned as the Scarab, and when legislation finally
ended this unusual type of commercial vehicle, over
20,000 had been built.

Scammell became important makers of dumptrucks
for the construction and quarrying industries and were
joined by AEC in 1957 with their six-wheel Dumptruk.
From 1959 a massive 340 bhp 50-ton (gross) four-
wheel version was offered. When Aveling-Barford, the
long-established steam and diesel roller makers joined
Leyland, they took over the dumptruck interests of
Thornycroft, AEC, and Scammell.

Comparatively recent events and models at British
Leyland have been so varied it is impossible to do them

justice in a few words. The gas-turbine experiments in
Leyland trucks in the late 'sixties; the appearance of
Alvis as a maker of specialised off-road vehicles, and
the birth of the Leyland National bus in 1970 must be
mentioned. Today all the British Leyland goods' and
passenger vehicles bear the names AEC, Scammell,
Leyland, or Aveling-Barford. Yet these names are
really the tip of an iceberg containing virtually the entire
history of the British heavy-vehicle industry. Leyland
companies were amongst the first in the field and in
almost every case were the first in Britain to introduce
important features to goods' and heavy passenger
vehicles that we take for granted today; low-frame
buses, diesel engines, heavy articulated lorries, rigid
six-wheelers, all-wheel-drive vehicles, disc brakes, air
suspension, and many, many more.

The histories of British Leyland and of the bus and
truck industry in Britain are inseparably intertwined.

# INDEX